Contents

Introduction

In any society there is conflict: different people want different things. Somehow these differences must be resolved. Sometimes conflicts can be resolved by peaceful means – such as bargaining – but sometimes they cannot. When two people cannot resolve their differences by peaceful means, they fight against each other. When two states cannot resolve their differences peacefully, they go to **war**.

British painter Abraham Cooper (1787–1868) imagined this combat between King Richard I of England and the Kurdish general Salah-al-din during the Third Crusade (1187–1192).

Sometimes conflicts are about resources – money, for example, or land or minerals. In 1960–63 the Congolese province of Katanga fought a war with Congo's government over who would control Katanga's rich mineral resources, including extensive supplies of copper and cobalt. Sometimes conflicts are about ideas. In 1096, Europe was swept up in the fervour of crusades – Christian holy wars. Christian kings, knights and even children went to war with people whose ideas about God differed from theirs. But these were often also about land – the crusaders wanted to take the Christian holy places in and near Jerusalem from the Muslims. The crusades began with attacks on French and German Jews who, like the Muslims, had religious beliefs and customs that differed from those of the Christians. The crusaders went on to kill Christians in the Middle East who were religiously and culturally different from Christians in Western Europe.

Ethnic differences

Some conflicts have nothing to do with what people think or want. Sometimes people fight about who they are. A group of people who share a common culture and language, or who believe they share a common ancestry, is known as an **ethnic group**. Ethnic identity is often a positive thing, giving rise to special arts, literature, clothing and spirituality or religion. Sometimes, however, ethnic groups conflict with one another simply because they are different.

Guerrilla warfare

For many people, war tends to be thought of as a series of large **battles** fought on battlefields. But some groups do not have the resources to make war in this way, although they still seek to resolve conflict with violence. When these groups fight against a stronger, **regular army** or attack important economic targets, such as power stations or railway lines, they are called '**guerrilla**' fighters. (Guerrilla is a Spanish word meaning 'little war').

❝War is merely the continuation of politics by other means.❞

The German philosopher Carl von Clausewitz (1780–1831) maintained that war was just a way to achieve political aims by using violence in an organized way.

Some groups go beyond guerrilla warfare and seek to use violence against people who cannot fight back. Someone who sets out to attack ordinary people to achieve an aim is called a **terrorist**.

The development of war

There have probably been **wars** as long as civilization has existed. The Bible tells of wars that happened more than 3000 years ago. In ancient Greece, between 479 BCE and 323 BCE, powerful cities were only able to go to war with each other in a very limited way. These cities were dominated by wealthy farmers, and they went to war to achieve the goals of these powerful men. To protect their interests, the farmers had to plan their methods of fighting carefully. For instance, they could not give weapons to their slaves, or the slaves might use these weapons to overthrow the farmers. The cities therefore had to content themselves with small armies of farmers. The farmers did not want to share power with craftsmen and labourers. To avoid this, they required all soldiers to wear a very expensive type of bronze breastplate called a 'hoplon'. As the wealthy farmers were the only people who could afford to buy armour, they were the only people who could carry weapons and hold power.

Battles and battlefields

The soldiers were called '**hoplites**', from the Greek word meaning 'hoplon-wearer'. Because hoplites were farmers, and farmers work hard, they could not spend a great deal of time practising their military skills. So when hoplites went

This Greek soldier from the 5th century BCE is putting on his armour, with the shoulder pieces standing up behind him.

to war, they could only do one thing: stand beside each other in line to fight. Because their armour was so heavy, they could not fight for long, so they fought short **battles**.

The hoplites could only fight in lines, so they needed to fight in broad, flat places. The first thing they did when they arrived to fight their enemies was to seek out a field for battle. With a few exceptions, hoplites always fought their battles on battlefields. This gives us our modern idea of war as a series of battles fought quickly on battlefields.

The two opposing hoplite armies would try to push each other off the field of battle. Eventually, one of the armies would become exhausted or frightened, and would try to run from the field. The

soldiers would drop their heavy armour and weapons and run back to their town or ships. The other army would build a great pile of all the discarded weapons and armour, called a trophy. This was a signal to the Greek gods that one side had won and the other had lost. This gives us the idea that wars are decided by battle, and that at the end one side has lost the battle while the other has won it.

❝... the Greeks... have senseless wars in which the two sides decide it is time they had a battle, march out to the smoothest and most convenient ground and proceed to butcher one another.❞

Herodotus, Greek historian of the 5th century BCE

This is a carefully made copy of a Greek warship of the 4th and 5th centuries BCE.

Land and ideas

In history, land has often been seen as a far more important measure of wealth than money. A **war** about land is straightforward because a piece of land is something everyone can see or understand. But sometimes wars about land are also about ideas.

For example, beginning in 1096, Christian rulers from Europe participated in crusades. These wars were mainly meant to win control over Christian holy places. This makes the crusades seem like wars of religious ideas, but many rulers actually participated in order to gain land for their families.

In contrast, from 1340, English and French kings fought wars over control of France. When the old French royal house died out in 1328, the kings of England claimed to be the rightful kings of France as well. The wars they fought, known together as the Hundred Years' War, were purely about which king would control France.

A 13th century manuscript painting of knights setting out on the First Crusade, 200 years earlier.

The Albigensian Crusade

In 1209 the Pope declared a crusade against the **Cathar** religion, which was strongest in Languedoc, to the south of France. The Christian church treated the Cathar religion as an incorrect or **heretical** set of beliefs called 'Albigensianism', after the town of Albi where the Cathars were strong. The Pope declared that people who joined the Christian army to fight the Cathars would earn God's forgiveness for their past sins.

The beautiful Languedoc city of Carcassone was a Cathar stronghold during the Albigensian Crusade.

After years of warfare, a new pope convinced a new king of France to join the Albigensian Crusade. In May 1226 King Louis VIII accepted a large cash gift from the Church and led an army southwards. For the king of France, who did not rule Languedoc, this was an opportunity to seize control of a large area of rich farmland while also creating a feeling of unity among northern French Christians. By the time the Crusade ended in 1229, Louis had gone from being the ruler only of parts of northern France to being the ruler of territories running from the English Channel to the Mediterranean.

The Albigensian Crusade shows that the same war can be fought over both territory and ideas. While the popes had started the Albigensian Crusade as a war of ideas, Louis had fought for land, to bring more of France under his control, and for money.

Industry and war

The first rifles, produced in the 16th century, were handmade by master craftsmen and their apprentices. Only rich men could afford to buy these weapons, and they were certainly not prepared to send them off to **war** with soldiers who might break or lose them. Instead, soldiers were armed with cheaper but less accurate muskets. However, by the end of the American Civil War, in 1865, hundreds of thousands of soldiers were armed with rifles.

Revolution

The event that brought about this change between the 16th and 19th centuries was the **Industrial Revolution**. In the 19th century, one worker at a machine could produce many rifles, whereas before it had taken many craftsmen to make one weapon. The industrialization of Europe changed other aspects of war too. In 1812, soldiers of the French emperor, Napoleon Bonaparte, marched to war along the tree-shaded avenues of rural France. In 1870, Bonaparte's nephew, Napoleon III and his men boarded

trains to war. For the first time in history, huge numbers of troops could be moved around very quickly, and **telegraph** wires along the railway tracks enabled generals to stay in touch with their political leaders.

In 1814 there was no reason to have an army of a million soldiers – no army could buy a million weapons! But by 1914 a million rifles, tents, water-bottles and pairs of shoes could be quickly made in factories. A million men could be fed, clothed, armed and transported to battlefields.

Soldiers fighting with rifles in the American Civil War.

World War One

When Austria-Hungary attacked Serbia in 1914, Russia mobilized its vast army to help its **ally**, Serbia. When the messages began to go out over Russian telegraph wires to summon **reservists** to railway stations, Germany (Austria-Hungary's ally) reacted. Expecting a short war, the Germans declared war on Russia and Russia's ally, France. The German Kaiser (emperor) expected his war with France to take two or three weeks.

The Kaiser was wrong. Between 1914 and 1918, 20 million people died in the industrialized World War One. Germany had tremendous industrial potential, but so did the British and French empires. In 1917 the USA entered the war on the side of Britain and France, lending them its vast industrial output.

After four years of war, German **civilians** were starving and the army was running out of food and equipment. German farmers could not compete with the farmers of the British Empire, France and the USA. German factories could not compete with British, French and US industry. The war could not be sustained, and Germany asked for an armistice (a **ceasefire**).

World War Two

World **War** Two (1939–45) was fought between two alliances. Japan, Germany, Italy and their **allies** sought to build empires ruled over by **dictators**. Britain, France, Russia, the USA (after 1941) and their allies sought to stop them. Like World War One, this was an industrialized war; but it was far more a war of ideas than the first war had been.

The Cold War

Even before the end of World War Two, the uneasy relationship between the Western allies (notably France, the USA and the countries of the British **Commonwealth**) and the **Soviet Union** was worsening. Soon the Western allies squared up to face their wartime ally, the Soviet Union, now ruled by the dictator Joseph Stalin.

Stalin was afraid that the Western allies would join together to attack the Soviet Union. The West, on the other hand, feared the spread of **communism**. Each side thought the other wanted to rule the world.

During World War Two, the Western allies had developed the first **atomic** weapons, with the Soviet Union following close behind. Atomic weapons were far more destructive than the **chemical weapons** that had been used

German civilians clamber out of air-raid shelters during the Allied invasion of Germany in World War Two.

during previous wars. As each side made newer, more powerful atomic weapons, the other side kept pace. The aircraft and missiles became so fast that each side was prepared to attack the other on a warning, without waiting for confirmation that the other side was attacking. Like the great European powers in 1914, the two sides were closely matched and capable of enormous destruction.

By the 1970s, each side had amassed enough weapons to destroy the other side several times over. According to the scientist Carl Sagan, the destruction of a nuclear war could result in great clouds of dust blocking the Sun's light from the entire Earth, with a dark 'nuclear winter' destroying all life on the planet.

This distrust between East and West became known as the 'Cold War'. Both the Soviet Union and the Western allies knew, however, that if they went to war the ensuing devastation would destroy both sides. This idea was called 'Mutually Assured Destruction' or 'MAD' and it ensured that, although the two sides prepared for nearly 35 years to fight World War Three, they never actually did so.

Although the USA and the Soviet Union could not safely fight each other during the Cold War, they sometimes allowed their allies to go to war. In 1973, for example, Egypt and Syria (supported by the Soviet Union) went to war with Israel (supported by the USA). The Cold War continued until the collapse of the Soviet Union in 1989.

❝I know not with what weapons World War Three will be fought, but World War Four will be fought with sticks and stones.❞

Scientist and inventor Albert Einstein (1879–1955), predicting the impact of a possible nuclear war on humanity.

This test of a nuclear weapon shows the 'mushroom cloud' that rises over the blast.

The Vietnam War

From the early 1960s, the anti-communist government of South Vietnam was in danger of falling to a communist **guerrilla** movement. Many Vietnamese people, from North and South, agreed with the communists' goal of unifying Vietnam and were not interested in the politics of **communism** and **capitalism**.

The US government sent advisors to help teach the South Vietnamese soldiers to do their jobs. As the **war** started to go against South Vietnam, the USA, with help from South Korea and Australia, sent more soldiers and equipment until, by 1965, they were full participants in the war.

Although US decision-makers tried hard to limit the Vietnam War, for soldiers like this US machine gunner and his Vietnamese communist enemies the war brought unlimited danger.

These Vietnamese communist fighters, taken prisoner by US Marines, are being marched into captivity.

The USA was very careful about its involvement in the Vietnam War. It was concerned that if the war became too fierce, it could involve other states – even the **Soviet Union**. The USA was determined not to allow the war in Vietnam to turn the Cold War into World War Three.

The United States government made every effort to keep the war from affecting daily life in the USA. When they discovered that the North Vietnamese received their supplies by a road that ran through neighbouring Laos and Cambodia, the Americans took care to attack the road in secret, because they did not want to draw more countries into the conflict. The USA did not bring all their military might to bear on Vietnam, and did not use their nuclear weapons. They stated clearly that they only wished to help preserve South Vietnam, and did not wish to take over North Vietnam.

However, in 1968, the Americans began to feel that they were no longer winning the war in Vietnam. Some US decision-makers feared that if they continued to fight in Vietnam, the public would demand that they send more soldiers, use more powerful weapons, and conduct a bigger war in order to win. This, they believed, could lead to World War Three with the Soviet Union, a disaster they were desperate to avoid.

Instead, the USA made the South Vietnamese try harder to defend themselves, so that the American troops could leave. By 1973, the last American soldiers had left Vietnam. But even with a new ruler, the South Vietnamese could not resist the popularity and military competence of the communists, and in 1975 Vietnam was unified under a communist government. The special conditions of the Cold War had helped to create a complex and costly war in Vietnam.

Regulars and irregulars

Soldiers who fight for their country, are paid and who are expected to follow rules, are called 'regulars'. This term comes from the Latin word *regula*, which means 'rule'. Some regular soldiers are 'conscripts', in other words they are drafted or 'conscripted' into the army for a set period of time. Other regular soldiers are professionals: they expect soldiering to be their career, and intend to continue in the profession for many years.

Shaka Zulu

Regular armies are not simply a feature of Western warfare. The powerful leader, Shaka Zulu (1785–1828) created a regular army which he used to lay claim to the Zulu state in southern Africa. Shaka's soldiers were expected to follow rules. They were all required to live together in the same house, although each regiment of men had its own living space. All the soldiers' weapons were identical. Soldiers who broke the rules were punished with death.

Shaka's 'Zulu' army had an advantage over warriors from other African clans and nations. Much of this advantage in **war** was because it was a regular army in a region in which most armies were not made up of regular soldiers. Because Shaka had a regular army, he was able to create the vast state of Zululand, which lasted for just over 50 years.

These officer cadets of the United States Military Academy at West Point are celebrating the end of their training to be regular army officers.

Soldiers who are not regulars are sometimes called '**irregulars**'. During the period of British rule in India (1755–1947), for example, the British found that, although some tribes of Indian horsemen made excellent soldiers, they were not happy under the strict discipline of the regular army. These men were recruited as irregular **cavalry**, and had their own rules. Irregulars were often more effective at certain jobs than regular cavalry soldiers.

> **❝The conventional army loses if it does not win. The guerrilla wins if he does not lose.❞**
>
> Henry Kissinger, then US National Security Advisor, January 1969

'RPG kids'

Regular soldiers do not always have the advantage over irregulars. When Israel invaded Lebanon in 1982, they marched with a regular army. They had the very best of modern equipment and training, and expected their heavily armoured tanks and armoured personnel carriers (APCs) to protect them from attack.

However, as the Israelis passed through Lebanese villages they found themselves attacked by young Palestinian fighters armed with simple anti-tank weapons, in the form of rocket-propelled grenades (RPGs). These 'RPG kids' would drive their ordinary **civilian** vehicles out of alleyways, and before the Israelis could react, would fire at Israeli vehicles and then disappear into the maze of back streets.

These irregular fighters walk through the streets of Beirut, Lebanon, in 1982. The long pipes they carry are RPG launchers.

Wars between armies

Some modern **wars**, like ancient wars, have been wars between armies. When the United States went to war with Spain in 1898, the American army and navy fought what is called a conventional war: the armies of the two nations faced each other in **battles**, and the navies faced each other at sea. When the United States went to war again almost 20 years later in 1917, their army joined the armies of the Allies in World War One to fight conventional war against the German and Austria-Hungarian armies.

The Falkland Islands War

The British call a small group of islands in the South Atlantic the Falklands. Argentina knows them as the Malvinas. Since the early 19th century, Argentina and Britain had both laid claim to the islands. For years, negotiations were carried out about the future of the islands, but neither side would give up its claim.

In 1982, with Argentina's corrupt dictatorship facing opposition at home, the country's military leaders decided to go to war. They thought that war would unite the people of Argentina against a common enemy. Instead of hating and resenting the cruel and ruthless government and its secret police, the Argentinean people would instead focus their hatred and resentment on the British.

Invasion and response

When the Argentines invaded the islands, on 2 April 1982, the British response was quick. Ships packed with soldiers set sail for the South Atlantic. The British government declared that any unfriendly ships near the islands would be sunk by Britain's Royal Navy. While the British ships sailed slowly across thousands of miles of sea, the Argentines prepared to defend the islands.

These British regular soldiers are marching across East Falkland island towards Stanley, the capital of the Falklands. All the British and some of the Argentine soldiers in the war were professionals.

A conventional war

When the British ships arrived, the war began in earnest. Argentine aircraft sank British warships and **merchant ships**; British aircraft sank Argentine warships and merchant ships. The soldiers of the British army fought with and killed Argentine soldiers, and Argentine soldiers fought with and killed British soldiers. After 72 days, the commander of the Argentine forces surrendered, and both he and his army were permitted to return home. Argentina had failed to win the islands from British rule.

A Greek commander of the Classical period would have understood the war completely. The ships had changed, the weapons had changed; but the war was the same: conventional war between two opposing armies.

Weapons of mass destruction

All weapons cause damage to their victims – that is what weapons are meant to do. Some weapons of **war** are capable of killing masses of people at once, with no distinction between soldiers and **civilians** or between important targets and unimportant ones. These are called 'weapons of mass destruction'.

Poison gas and atomic bombs

Chemical weapons are poisons, usually poison gas or mist. During World War One, both sides developed poison gas weapons and began using them in 1915. Another weapon of mass destruction introduced during World War One was **biological warfare**. This attacks the enemy by infecting them with a disease, for example, anthrax.

During World War Two, scientists from around the world developed the **atomic bomb**. The first atomic bombs were tested and used in the summer of 1945. The first **hydrogen bombs** were tested in 1952, but they have never been used in war.

Weapons of mass destruction have been used recently, for example, during the Iran-Iraq War (1980–88). In this war both the Iranians and the Iraqis began to use poison gas against each other. In 1987 the Iraqi government began using poison gas as part of a campaign against the Kurdish people in northern Iraq, killing civilian adults and children.

Extremist groups

Although there is concern that countries may use weapons of mass destruction against their enemies, threats from non-state groups could be more dangerous. While even **dictators** may be deterred from using weapons of mass destruction if they know that their enemies might use similar weapons in return, some extremist groups are harder to threaten.

Aum Shinrikyo is a religious **cult** based in Japan. The group believes that the world will end soon, and that it is a good idea to help the world end sooner. There is evidence to suggest that members of Aum Shinrikyo released microbes which cause anthrax and botulism (two deadly diseases) in Japan in 1993. In 1995 the group attempted to commit mass murder by introducing a poison gas into Tokyo's underground railway system. Twelve people were killed by the gas and about 5000 were injured.

The USA is a powerful state, and it has many enemies. People who feel that they have no other way to strike against the USA might smuggle nuclear weapons into the country to cause death, radiation poisoning and fear. The threat of such action by extremist groups has led the USA to invest in equipment that can detect small amounts of nuclear material.

On 6 August 1945 a single atomic bomb from a single aircraft devastated the city of Hiroshima in Japan. Three days later, another bomb destroyed the Japanese city of Nagasaki. On 14 August 1945, Japan surrendered.

Ethnic and religious conflicts

An **ethnic group** is made up of people who share a history and culture. Often an ethnic group will also share a language, a national costume or a religion. Sometimes an ethnic group will have a particularly close tie to a piece of land. One example is the Basque ethnic group in Spain. Some Basques insist that they must have a state of their own. A very small group of Basques conduct a campaign of violent **terrorism** against the Spanish government in support of ethnic self-rule.

Kosovo

People move from place to place, so the same piece of land can be important to more than one ethnic group. The province of Kosovo is in the state of Serbia in the former Yugoslavia. It is settled mostly by ethnic Albanians, who speak the Albanian language, write with the Roman alphabet and are mostly Muslims. The province also has a population of Serbs. They are ethnic Slavs, who speak Serbo-Croatian, write with the Cyrillic alphabet and are mostly Orthodox Christians.

In 1389, a Serb army fought against the armies of the Turkish sultan in Kosovo. The site of this battle is important to Serbs as a symbol of their fight against the Turks, and also of the Christians' fight against Muslims for control of the region.

The policeman on the left is fighting with an ethnic Albanian rioter in Kosovo province in 1998.

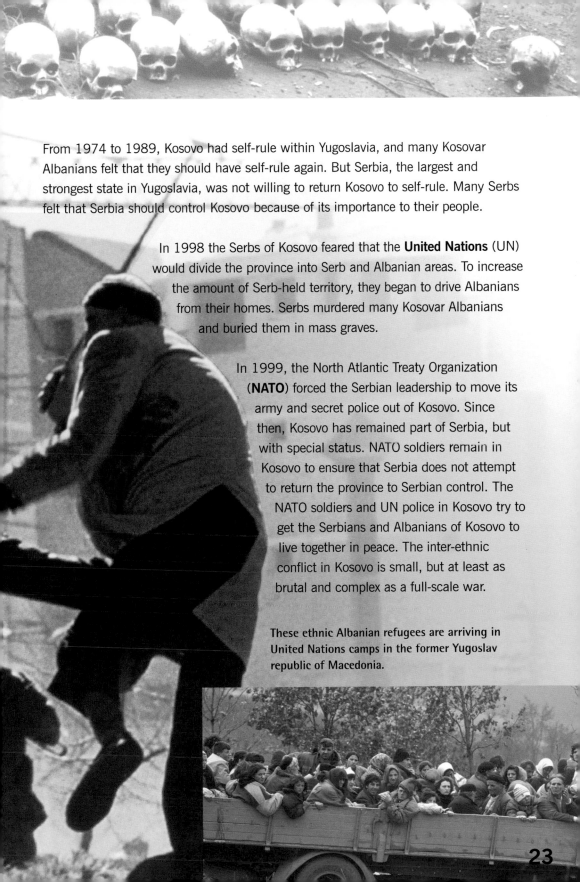

From 1974 to 1989, Kosovo had self-rule within Yugoslavia, and many Kosovar Albanians felt that they should have self-rule again. But Serbia, the largest and strongest state in Yugoslavia, was not willing to return Kosovo to self-rule. Many Serbs felt that Serbia should control Kosovo because of its importance to their people.

In 1998 the Serbs of Kosovo feared that the **United Nations** (UN) would divide the province into Serb and Albanian areas. To increase the amount of Serb-held territory, they began to drive Albanians from their homes. Serbs murdered many Kosovar Albanians and buried them in mass graves.

In 1999, the North Atlantic Treaty Organization (**NATO**) forced the Serbian leadership to move its army and secret police out of Kosovo. Since then, Kosovo has remained part of Serbia, but with special status. NATO soldiers remain in Kosovo to ensure that Serbia does not attempt to return the province to Serbian control. The NATO soldiers and UN police in Kosovo try to get the Serbians and Albanians of Kosovo to live together in peace. The inter-ethnic conflict in Kosovo is small, but at least as brutal and complex as a full-scale war.

These ethnic Albanian refugees are arriving in United Nations camps in the former Yugoslav republic of Macedonia.

War crimes

Acts that are illegal in peacetime, such as shooting or bombing, are made legal in wartime. As long as a soldier commits the act, shooting an enemy soldier in the head is not murder; hitting an enemy soldier in the head is not assault. In fact, soldiers in wartime are often rewarded for doing things that they would be punished for doing in peacetime. Some deeds are, however, so horrible that they are considered crimes even in wartime. A **war crime** is killing or destruction which breaks the laws of **war**, and which is not required to achieve military aims.

Genocide

The laws of war govern the way soldiers behave when fighting. They also govern the treatment of **civilians**, prisoners, medics and property. During World War Two, Germany broke the laws of war by committing **genocide** (mass murder) against Jews and other **ethnic groups**. After the war, German leaders were put on trial in Nuremberg, where a **tribunal** (court) ruled on whether each one was guilty of war crimes. Some of those found guilty were hanged and some were imprisoned.

Some war criminals escaped from Germany before they could be put on trial. Adolf Eichmann, one of the men who planned the genocide of Europe's Jews, fled to Argentina. The State of Israel (created shortly after World War Two as a homeland for the Jews) tracked him down and smuggled him to Jerusalem where he stood trial for war crimes. The Israeli court convicted Eichmann and he was hanged in 1962.

Nazi mass murderer Adolf Eichmann stands to hear an Israeli court announce that he has been found guilty of war crimes.

❝I think that technologies are morally neutral until we apply them. It's only when we use them for good or for evil that they become good or evil.❞

Author William Gibson, 23 November 1994.

Massacres

In 1982, when Ariel Sharon was Israel's defence minister, Israel invaded Lebanon. One of the main reasons for the invasion was to help put a Lebanese **militia** called the Christian Falange in control of Lebanon. This, Sharon hoped, would end Palestinian attacks on Israel from Lebanon.

The Israelis took control of several Palestinian **refugee** camps in Lebanon. The Christian Falange stormed into the Sabra and Shatila refugee camps near Beirut and **massacred** between 700 and 800 people. Among them were many Palestine Liberation Organization (**PLO**) and militia fighters, but the number also included 15 women and 20 children.

An Israeli commission of inquiry concluded that Sharon had some responsibility for the massacre, because Israeli troops did not stop the killing, but it decided that he was not a war criminal. The Christian Falangist leader Elie Hobeika, who probably was responsible for the massacre, was never charged or punished. He lived in Lebanon for many years until he was murdered in 2002.

Recently, war crimes tribunals have met to try people accused of crimes against humanity in Rwanda and the former Yugoslavia. The tribunals have found it difficult to compel (force) people to stand trial. The **United Nations** managed to bring former Yugoslav president Slobodan Milosevic to trial; but it is harder to find the people who ordered and carried out the killings.

The consequences of conflict

For the people who live in a **war** zone, war does not simply go away when a **ceasefire** is declared. It is almost 100 years since World War One littered the fields of Belgium with craters. Yet every year Belgian farmers' ploughs turn up bodies, equipment and, worst of all, unexploded **shells**. Often the shells are still dangerous, and army experts are called to destroy them.

Landmines

Landmines are explosive devices that are buried underground. When a person or a vehicle triggers the mine, it explodes. Small mines – called antipersonnel mines – can kill a person. Larger mines can destroy vehicles, even tanks.

> **Landmines are uniquely savage in the history of modern conventional warfare not only because of their appalling individual impact, but also their long-term social and economic destruction.**

Graça Machel, UN Secretary-General's Expert on the Impact of Armed Conflict on Children, in the Machel Report, 1994.

When **regular armies** finish fighting, their engineers are expected to find and remove their landmines. **Irregular** armies are not so careful. Today thousands of landmines remain in former war zones. Animals sometimes trigger landmines by walking across them. Children sometimes trigger them while playing. It is estimated that 30–40 per cent of landmine victims in the world are less than fifteen years of age.

In 1996 there were an estimated 10 million landmines in Cambodia. These young Cambodians (below) are victims of mine explosions.

Cluster bombs

Other dangerous devices litter former battlefields. Cluster bombs are made up of many small 'bomblets'. Each of these is filled with explosive, and when they explode the damage is greater than that of a single bomb. Sometimes bomblets are defective, and they fail to explode when they are supposed to. Cluster bombs resemble a small football, and when children find them they often play with them. The bomb may then detonate (explode), wounding or killing the children.

Toxic smoke billows from the oil wells of Kuwait, blown up by retreating Iraqis at the end of the Gulf War in 1991.

Dangerous chemicals

Chemicals used in explosives or in fuels can often be left in war zones. Some people have claimed that dust from the bullets used in some guns during the Gulf War (1990–91) has made them ill. Some scientists suggest that the insect spray used to prevent the spread of disease in military camps poisoned soldiers who were fighting in the Gulf War.

In war, many important targets can involve chemicals. Explosives may hit factories where weapons and explosives are made, or where consumer goods like plastics or aluminium are produced. Chemicals used in manufacturing or toxic waste products can be spread over wide areas, poisoning the air and water.

Damage to the environment can hurt people directly. In many parts of the world, a single cow or sheep is an important part of a family's wealth. If it is killed by a landmine or poisoned by chemicals released in an explosion, a family can be ruined – sometimes brought to starvation.

Casualties

Civilian casualties

War brings disaster to people who are not involved in the fighting. Young people are the next generation of earners and providers. If they are killed or maimed in war, then their families can suffer deprivation.

By 1915, British soldiers had learned to rush out of the trenches in little groups called 'blobs' in the hope of avoiding wounding or death.

This boy, being carried to safety by a Red Cross worker, was wounded in fighting between two **guerrilla** groups in Colombia.

On 1 July 1916, 753 men of the Royal Newfoundland Regiment marched across 500 metres of open ground in France. They were part of the British army that was conducting the Battle of the Somme against the Germans in World War One. The Newfoundlanders met with a wall of German machine-gun fire. Within half an hour, 710 of the men had been killed, wounded or were missing.

Newfoundland is an island off the coast of Canada, now part of the Canadian province of Newfoundland and Labrador. At the start of World War One, Newfoundland's population was about 250,000. When Britain became involved in the war, Newfoundland was expected to contribute to the war effort, and 5482 men and women went overseas to help. More than a third of Newfoundland's young men joined the armed forces to fight. During the four years of the war, 1500 Newfoundlanders were killed and 2300 were wounded.

The special conditions of World War One resulted in a rapid and devastating spread of disease. Measles, mumps and pneumonia rampaged through the units of soldiers living close together in the dirty conditions of trenches and troopships. Eventually about 7500 Newfoundlanders would die of diseases contracted as a result of the war.

The lost generation

Newfoundland was profoundly affected by the loss of so many of its young people, especially the young male soldiers. The tightly-knit island community had lost about 9000 people in the space of five years. Until new families could be raised there was a shortage of people to do important jobs, a shortage of parents for children and a shortage of husbands and wives for young people growing up.

Worldwide, the generation of World War One was sometimes referred to as 'the Lost Generation', a term first used by the American writer Gertrude Stein. She was referring to the people who had been lost in the war, but also to the people who had survived and who lived with the loss of their friends and families.

Refugees

However they may feel about the reasons for **war**, ordinary people do not feel safe when bullets are whizzing past them and into their houses. Often people must move away from a war zone for their own safety. When people leave their houses they become **refugees**. They need a place to sleep, and a source of food and water. The **United Nations** High Commissioner for Refugees and other United Nations organizations establish camps for refugees and try to provide for their basic needs.

Ethnic cleansing

During the Bosnian Civil War (1991–95), Bosnian Muslims, Serbs and Croats wanted to create areas with people from only one **ethnic group**. In a process called 'ethnic cleansing', ethnic groups deliberately destroyed the homes of people from other ethnic groups in order to make them refugees. If they did not leave, they were often attacked or murdered. The refugees had to move elsewhere in Bosnia – sometimes elsewhere in Europe. This **transfer of population** is illegal under international law, but it is difficult to prevent.

During the Israeli War of Independence (1948–49), many Arabs living in formerly British-ruled Palestine left their homes. Some people left because they heard broadcasts on Arab radio stations telling them to leave temporarily, and promising they could come back when the war was over. Some left because they feared that the Israelis would harm them. Others left because they knew that, in war, innocent **civilians** are often killed or injured by accident.

When the war was over, the Israelis refused to allow the Arab refugees to return to their homes. They told them to settle in the Arab sector of Palestine, then controlled by Jordan and Egypt.

The building of permanent homes for Palestinian refugees is illegal under international law because it represents a transfer of population. Arab countries have been unwilling to give homes to the Palestinians, largely because it is useful for them to have a large population of refugees demanding the destruction of Israel. The United Nations Relief and Works Agency for Palestine has provided refugee camps for the Palestinian refugees, and many have lived in these camps ever since leaving Palestine.

This woman from Khan Younis in the Palestinian Authority's Gaza Strip is old enough to have known British, Egyptian and Israeli occupation.

Terrorism

Terrorism is the purposeful murder and maiming of the innocent and the defenceless to inspire fear in order to achieve political goals. A **guerrilla** or a soldier might accidentally kill innocent people, but **terrorists** *plan* to kill people who are not a direct threat to them.

Terrorists are people who find that their goals cannot be achieved through peaceful means or even through guerrilla warfare. Often their aims cannot be achieved at all. Because they cannot gain support for their aims through positive means, they gain attention and support through negative means. They kill and maim people in order to inspire fear. Because people are less frightened by attacks against soldiers, who have weapons and can defend themselves, terrorists choose to attack **civilians**.

The terrorist relies on the media to spread fear. If people did not know that the violence took place, then they would not be afraid. To the media, however, terrorism is news, and it is their duty to report it. Some governments, such as that of Britain, do not allow the media to report failed terrorist incidents or to broadcast terrorist demands. These governments hope that, without publicity, the terrorists will fail in their aims.

Security forces survey the damage after terrorists of the 'Real IRA' exploded a bomb in Omagh, Northern Ireland in 1998, killing 29 civilians.

❝Kill one, frighten a thousand.❞

Sun Tzu, Chinese general and philosopher of war, c.500 BCE

Some governments use terrorists to attack their enemies and to manipulate world affairs. This is called 'state-sponsored terrorism'. Some state sponsors of terrorism provide money or training for terrorists and allow them openly to set up offices and recruit others. They provide a safe place where terrorists can hide when other governments are pursuing them.

Some criminals use terrorism to frighten governments into allowing them to operate businesses. For example, the drug producers of Colombia use terrorism to cripple the nation's criminal justice system by murdering and intimidating people employed in it. This is called 'narco-terrorism'.

There is a slogan among those who support terrorists: 'One man's terrorist is another man's freedom fighter.' This slogan says that because terrorists often claim to fight for 'freedom', they should be thought better than ordinary criminals. Those who oppose terrorists have two replies. First, they point out that terrorism can be a means of achieving any number of goals: freedom, power or money. Second, they point out that while a very few people have used terror to achieve freedom for themselves and others, most terrorists fight for their own power and influence.

33

Al-Qaeda

From 1978, a **communist** government controlled Afghanistan, supported from late 1979 by the army of the **Soviet Union**. People from around the Muslim world came to help Afghans who fought to get the Soviets out. These resistance groups were supported by the USA and other countries. One of the resistance leaders was Osama bin Laden of Saudi Arabia. He was an organizer and a wealthy man who was able to channel money from other wealthy men to support his cause.

When the Soviet Union withdrew its army from Afghanistan in 1989, many of the resistance fighters found it difficult to go home and return to normal life. Some missed the feeling of power that came from killing; some missed the feeling of freedom that came from living in the hills. Others missed the sense of mission that came with fighting to eject non-Muslims from a Muslim land. Although some of the fighters came from deprived backgrounds, many were wealthy young men used to money and privilege.

Osama bin Laden brought many of the fighters together to continue their violent way of life outside Afghanistan. They formed a new group which would seek to end American influence in Muslim countries and to destroy the State of Israel. Because they could not succeed by means of conventional **war**, they would fight with terror: they would kill Americans and Jews.

The group soon became known as 'al-Qaeda ul-Sullbah', Arabic for 'the firm base', or 'al-Qaeda' ('the base') for short. In 1998, bin Laden merged al-Qaeda with an Egyptian group called al-Jihad (meaning 'the holy war') which had similar goals. The new al-Qaeda was backed by many of the wealthy individuals who had supported them in their fight against the Soviet Union.

In 1998, al-Qaeda became known worldwide when it bombed American embassies in Africa, killing hundreds of people.

On 11 September 2001, civilian airliners were hijacked by members of al-Qaeda, who flew them into the World Trade Center (a large office complex in New York) and the Pentagon (the USA's defence headquarters in Washington DC). Thousands of ordinary people were killed. The USA and its **allies** responded by destroying al-Qaeda's bases in Afghanistan and by pledging to seek out and destroy **terrorism** everywhere.

Most Muslim people do not share al-Qaeda's devotion to religious terror and violence. Muslim leaders generally consider Islamic terrorism to be a corruption of Muslim beliefs.

On 11 September 2001, two hijacked passenger aircraft flew into the twin towers of New York's World Trade Center, causing mass death and destruction.

War and peace

A demonstration against the rearmament of Britain in 1936. The gas masks are a reminder of the gas warfare of World War One.

Civilized states hate going to **war**. War brings death, destruction and ruin. It is expensive and unpleasant. Failure in war can bring national embarrassment, as the USA found in the years after the war in Vietnam. Even success in war can lead to unexpected outcomes. US President George Bush was very popular at the time of the Gulf War, but only a few months later he was defeated in an election.

Many people believe that because war is horrible, it must be avoided at all costs. They believe that no matter how bad the alternative, war is always the wrong choice. This idea is known as pacifism. The horror of World War One made pacifism a popular idea in Europe. Millions of deaths in war had convinced many that anything was better than that. Then they faced the threat of Adolf Hitler and **Nazi Germany**.

Taking over Europe

Some Europeans in the 19th century imagined that they were part of an **ethnic group** called the 'Aryan race'. Long before Hitler became dictator of Germany in 1934, he planned to build a vast super-state for the Aryan race. The Aryans were, said Hitler and his followers, a race of rulers, and they would rule over all of Europe, using other 'inferior peoples' as their slaves.

When Hitler's Germany became strong enough, he began to take over other countries. In 1938, the Germans took over Austria. Later in the year, they invaded Czechoslovakia (now the Czech Republic and Slovakia). Britain and France were pledged to defend Czechoslovakia. Some people suggested that it was essential to stop Hitler; others pointed out that the only way to stop him was to go to war. The pacifist feeling in Europe said that anything was better than war, and even those who opposed Hitler were not united. So Hitler was allowed to take part of Czechoslovakia. This encouraged him to take the rest of Czechoslovakia, and to invade Poland the following year, thus starting World War Two.

In 1938 Germany was not strong enough to stand up to an alliance of Poland, Czechoslovakia, Britain and France. But Britain and France left Hitler alone in part because they were afraid to start a war. Their delays allowed Nazi Germany to become powerful enough to defeat Poland and France, and nearly cripple Britain. Hitler taught the nations of Europe that sometimes the only way to end a war is to fight a war.

Adolf Hitler (with hands on rail) at a Nazi rally in 1933, shortly before becoming Germany's dictator.

Unsafe haven – Srebrenica

In the summer of 1995, a group of nations was trying to keep the peace in the former Yugoslav republic of Bosnia-Hercegovina. The nations were armed, but they were not prepared to fight. In one case, not fighting gave us the **massacres** of Srebrenica.

During the Bosnian Civil War of 1991–95, Bosnia's Serb, Croat and Muslim **ethnic groups** fought each other, each trying to carve out a section of Bosnia for its own people. **Refugees** fled from the region into the

rest of Europe. The **United Nations** looked for places closer to home where people could safely go. In 1993, the United Nations Security Council declared the Bosnian town of Srebrenica to be a 'safe haven' where Bosniacs (Bosnian Muslims) could be safe from Croats and Serbs.

The Serbs wanted Srebrenica to be part of a Bosnian Serb area, and they wanted to get rid of the Bosniacs. In the summer of 1995, the Bosnian Serb army began **shelling** the town of

Srebrenica, 1996: an investigator marks each body in a mass grave with a red flag.

Srebrenica. The people of the town, including Bosniac soldiers and **civilians**, fled to nearby United Nations camps.

Several thousand Bosnian Muslims arrived at a Dutch **peacekeepers**' camp in the village of Potocari. Ratko Mladic, the commander of the Bosnian Serb army, told the Dutch and the Bosniacs that if the able-bodied men surrendered they would not be harmed. Outnumbered by the Serb army, the Dutch peacekeepers helped Mladic and his soldiers select the men and take them away. The peacekeepers then fled to their support base at Zagreb in Croatia. The Serb army took the Bosniac men away and massacred them.

Mladic and his soldiers then returned to Potocari and began killing more of the Bosniacs. They only stopped killing when the remaining Bosniacs begged to leave Srebrenica. It is estimated that six to eight thousand Bosniacs were killed in the Srebrenica area.

At Srebrenica, the peacekeepers did not fight: they were too few and too weak in the face of the Serbs. They kept the peace, and helped to arrange for the Bosniac men and boys to be sent to their deaths. The result was that the Bosnian

> **❝The... lesson of Srebrenica is that a deliberate and systematic attempt to terrorize, expel or murder an entire people must be met decisively with all necessary means....❞**
>
> The UN Secretary General's report on the fall of Srebrenica

Serbs were able to achieve their goals 'peacefully' – by mass murder.

The International Criminal **Tribunal** for the former Yugoslavia charged Ratko Mladic and his boss Radovan Karadzic with **genocide**, crimes against humanity and violating the laws of **war**. Yugoslavia and the Serb entity (presence) in Bosnia have refused to hand them over to the tribunal, so neither of them has stood trial for their crimes.

Peacekeepers are not supposed to take sides between the warring parties in a conflict, but neither are they supposed to remain neutral when it comes to deciding between right and wrong. On 16 April 2002, the Dutch government resigned in disgrace for failing to prevent the Srebrenica massacre.

Is war itself the enemy?

For hundreds of years people have agreed that **wars** are bad – but wars are still fought. Although medieval Christian culture taught that war was glorious and manly, some medieval churchmen suggested that wars should only be fought on certain days of the week. First, they said, there should be no fighting on Sundays – the Christian day of rest and worship. Then they extended this '**truce** of God' to Thursdays, Fridays and Saturdays. This did not bring peace: people just fought harder on Mondays, Tuesdays and Wednesdays.

A just war?

The Christian **theologian** and lawyer Thomas Aquinas (1226–74) said that only proper authorities, such as governments, should wage war. He also said that war was only to be waged in a **just cause** and with good intentions. In other words, leaders could only take their people to war to achieve peace and justice in the end.

Aquinas said that it is right to wage a **just war**. From Aquinas's time to World War One, war was considered to be simply a way for nations to settle their differences. After the tragedy of World War One, however, the nations of the world began to consider war itself to be wrong.

Efforts to ban war

In 1919, the **League of Nations** agreed that member states would try every possible alternative before going to war. In 1928, the Kellogg-Briand Pact was signed by the most powerful states in the world. The nations who agreed to the pact (agreement) said they would never go to war again. The pact effectively outlawed war. But every nation that agreed to the Kellogg-Briand Pact (except Ireland) went to war between 1939 and 1945.

When the **United Nations** was formed in 1945, its charter said that states no longer had the right to go to war: only the United Nations itself had the right. This charter has not succeeded in outlawing war. Since 1945, numerous member states of the United Nations have fought wars.

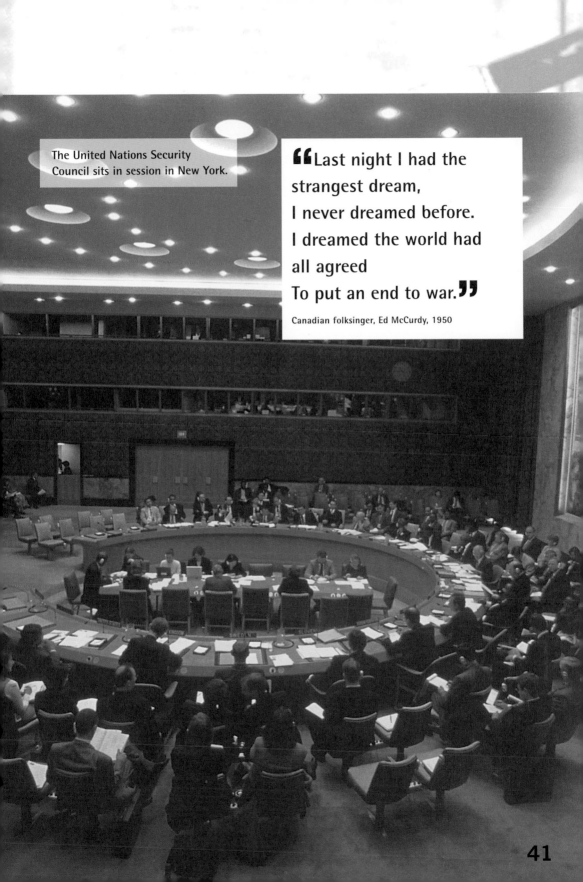

The United Nations Security Council sits in session in New York.

ffLast night I had the strangest dream,
I never dreamed before.
I dreamed the world had all agreed
To put an end to war.**ff**

Canadian folksinger, Ed McCurdy, 1950

41

Right and wrong in war

In 1604, the Dutch diplomat Hugo Grotius (1583–1645) published a book called *On the Law of War and Peace*. It suggested that a **war** did not only have to be just, it also had to be conducted in the right way. He suggested that there should be a set of rules that armies should follow when they are fighting.

Grotius said, for instance, that some things should not be destroyed in war. Fruit trees, churches and works of art should be left untouched. Prisoners should not be sold into slavery. These were the first workable rules to govern the conduct of war.

Saudi troops search a surrendering Iraqi soldier during the Gulf War, 1991.

The Geneva **conventions** (**treaties**), first agreed in 1864, and Hague conventions, which followed later, laid down a more complete set of rules for the conduct of war. The conventions protected noncombatants (people not involved in fighting), governed the treatment of prisoners and the wounded, and banned some weapons as barbaric. These conventions are not merely an attempt to make war more pleasant; they aim to keep the amount of unnecessary killing as small as possible. The conventions are enforced by courts made up of judges from different countries.

Surrender

In battle, if fighting is hopeless, soldiers must feel safe putting their hands up and surrendering. If they know that they can surrender without being robbed or murdered, they can give up rather than fight until they are killed. If surrendering is safe, then the fighting can end sooner.

To make surrender safe, the Hague Convention demands that when an army captures enemy soldiers, it should treat them well. Captured soldiers must give up their weapons, but they can keep their personal possessions. The army that captures them must feed and clothe them in the same manner that it would its own soldiers. When the war is over, the prisoners must be sent home as soon as possible.

The Red Cross

Jean Henri Dunant (1828–1910) was a Swiss lawyer who was on a business trip when he accidentally found himself at the **Battle** of Solferino in Italy. This battle, fought on 24 June 1859, was one of the bloodiest battles to have taken place in European history. On that one day, 6000 people were killed and 40,000 wounded. For three days and three nights, Dunant helped the local villagers care for wounded soldiers. He was horrified by the suffering caused by modern war, and sought to do something about it. In 1863, Dunant founded the Geneva Society for Public Welfare, which grew into the International Committee of the Red Cross (ICRC). The ICRC is an impartial, neutral and independent organization whose mission is to protect the lives and dignity of victims of war and internal violence and to provide them with assistance. It also tries to prevent suffering by promoting and strengthening humanitarian law and universal humanitarian principles.

Preventing conflicts

In 1945, following two world **wars**, nations no longer believed conflict to be a legitimate way of achieving their aims. When the **United Nations** was created, its aim was to 'spare future generations from the scourge of war'. The UN charter said that only the United Nations could use force to solve conflict.

Although the aims of the United Nations were international peace and security, the first large-scale United Nations operation was a war. In 1950, North Korea invaded South Korea, and the United Nations joined the war on the side of South Korea. The **Soviet Union**, a member of the United Nations, and China, then not a member, joined the war on the side of North Korea. The Korean War was fought from 1950 to 1953, and although there was a **ceasefire** in 1953, the war has never formally been ended.

A peacekeeping force

In 1956 the UN conducted its first **peacekeeping** operation. Britain and France had convinced Israel to go to war against Egypt in order to keep the European hold on the Suez Canal. The British and the French wanted to 'solve' the problem by sending their armies to separate the Egyptians and the Israelis. In the process, Britain and France would take over the part of Egypt that controlled the important Suez Canal.

It soon became clear that the Israelis and Egyptians wanted to stop fighting, but each side needed to be sure that if they stopped, the other side would stop too. What was needed was a neutral army to move between them, making it safe for both sides to stop fighting. The Egyptians, friends with the Soviet Union and China, would not accept a US peacekeeping force. The Israelis, friends with the USA and Europe, would not accept a Soviet peacekeeping force. No one would accept the British and the French, because they had planned the war in the first place.

Eventually, Lester Pearson, the Canadian foreign minister, suggested that a group of smaller countries could create a peacekeeping force under the UN banner. Both the Israelis and the Egyptians agreed. The first UN peacekeeping force consisted of soldiers from Canada, Sweden and other countries. Because the

Canadian soldiers wore berets that made them look very much like British soldiers, the UN arranged for their berets to be replaced with helmets painted sky blue. Ever since, when soldiers go on UN duty, they take off their national hats or helmets and replace them with the sky blue ones of the UN.

These people and vehicles were from different countries, but they were all part of the United Nations protection force in Sarajevo in 1995.

Other solutions

War is costly. The costs of war include people killed and injured, the resources spent on fighting, and resources destroyed by fighting. After wars are finished, humanitarian assistance and reconstruction can be expensive too. Preventing conflict is easier and less expensive than fighting wars.

The difficulty is that people go to war when they see no alternative. It is often hard to find alternatives and compromises that both sides of a conflict will accept. This has made it difficult to prevent wars by bargaining and discussion. The **United Nations** and regional bodies such as the European Union, the Organization for African Unity and the Organization of American States are dedicated to finding means to avoid war, but they are often unsuccessful.

Reducing the number of weapons

One means of preventing war is by agreeing to control **armament**. If states and groups keep their weapons stocks low enough, then their neighbours will feel more secure and will be less likely to consider war necessary. During the 1990s, the tensions of the Cold War were calmed by the Conventional Forces in Europe Treaty, which carefully controlled the number and type of weapons that the former Cold War enemies could keep in Europe.

If countries are to buy fewer weapons, they need to be convinced that their enemies will not attack them. If they join together to guarantee each other's security – by stationing multinational forces in danger zones, and by being open with one another – different nations can grow to feel more secure about their safety from attack.

Resolving conflicts

The best recent example of conflict resolution is South Africa. For many years, up until the 1990s, South Africa's white population had used racist laws to discriminate against the majority black population. The whites feared that they would become victims if free elections were held and a black government was voted in. The whites were

afraid that their human rights would be in danger, and so they clung to power and to the old racist laws.

The National Peace **Accord** of 14 September 1991 was designed to build confidence among white South Africans so that they would share power with the black majority and still feel safe enough to remain in and contribute to South Africa. The accord set up ways for people to solve their conflicts without violence. This built a feeling of security, which allowed the introduction of free and fair elections for the first time in South Africa in 1994.

Former South African president F. W. de Klerk (left) shakes hands with his successor, Nelson Mandela, after South Africa's 1994 elections.

War and conflict and you

Some young people learn about the realities of **war** and conflict by participating in sea, air or army cadet organizations. Cadets learn about leadership and adventure, but they also learn about soldiers and their way of life. This does not mean that they imagine war to be a pleasant or happy thing, just that it is something they want to learn about.

Organizations that seek to prevent war often encourage young people to participate. Many nations have **United Nations** associations, which sponsor programmes for young people. United Nations associations run Model United Nations events for young people, in which they learn about conflict resolution through role-playing and public speaking. Some even have summer camps where young people can come together to learn about the United Nations while also having fun. The United Nations Children's Fund, UNICEF, also has programmes to involve young people in its work.

Many national Red Cross societies have youth organizations that teach young people about Red Cross work, both domestic and international. Red Cross societies welcome young volunteers who can help relieve the suffering of war's victims. For example, within only a few months of the beginning of the Afghan War in 2001, American children had raised US$4 million for Afghan children in need.

People can use the Internet to learn more about conflict. The UN and other organizations have their own websites. Newspapers and broadcasters often provide links on their sites to those involved in the conflict. Regional organizations and **peacekeeping** forces usually have websites, and the people involved in the conflict often have websites of their own.

There are religious and political groups that campaign for conflict resolution and prevention. Other groups work to relieve suffering, especially for children. These groups often change with issues and conflicts of the moment. Parents and teachers can help you to find appropriate groups to study or join.

Two young Americans collect donations for the American Red Cross in the aftermath of the World Trade Center bombing in 2001. Collecting for charity is just one way young people can be Red Cross volunteers.

Facts and figures

Deaths in war – rough estimates

Number of **wars** fought in the 20th century..250

Source: Ruth L. Sivard, *World Military and Social Expenditure*

Number of people killed in war, 1901–2000....................87.5 million

Source: Zbigniew Brzezinski, *Out of Control: Global Turmoil on the Eve of the 21st Century*

Number of wars fought, 1945–95.....................................194

Source: Stiftung, Entwicklung und Frieden, *Global Trends 1998: Fakten, Analysen, Prognosen*

Number of people killed in war, 1945-95...........................45 million

Source: Jonathan Dean, Union of Concerned Scientists

Number of wars fought, 1990–95...93

Source: Dan Smith, *The State of War and Peace Atlas*

Number of people killed in war, 1990–95...........................5.5 million

Source: Dan Smith, *The State of War and Peace Atlas*

Money and war

Cost of fighting World War One...US$186,333,637,000

World War One

Number of soldiers mobilized........................65,038,810

Number killed and died of wounds 8,538,315

Number wounded............21,219,452

Number missing and taken prisoner............................7,750,919

Source: *Encyclopedia Britannica*

Terrorism

Number of people killed in international **terrorist** attacks, 1990–99 2527
Source: US State Department

Number of people reported missing or dead after 11 September 2001 attacks in the USA...............................2823
Source: *Washington Post*

Number of people killed by Palestinian terrorists in Israel in the fifteen years before the 1993 Israeli-Palestinian peace **accord** 254
Source: Israel Government Press Office

Number of people killed by Palestinian terrorists in Israel in the five years after the 1993 Israeli-Palestinian peace accord...256
Source: Israel Government Press Office

Mines – rough estimates

Number of people killed or maimed in landmine explosions worldwide in 1999.................................26,000
Number of people killed or maimed in landmine explosions worldwide in 2000.................................20,000

Number of people killed or maimed in landmine explosions worldwide in 2001.................................10,000
Cost of buying one landmine...US$3–30
Cost in US$ of removing one landmine $300–1000
Sources: US State Department and Landmine Monitor

Further information

Contacts in the UK

British Red Cross
9 Grosvenor Crescent
London SW1X 7EJ
Tel: 020 7201 5164
email: fmacleod@redcross.org.uk
http://www.redcross.org.uk/homepage.asp

United Nations Association UK
3 Whitehall Court
London SW1A 2EL
Tel: 020 7930 2931
email: info@una-uk.org
http://www.una-uk.org/

United Kingdom Committee for UNICEF
64–78 Kingsway
London EC2B 6NB
Tel: 020 7405 5592
email: info@unicef.org.uk
http://www/unicef.org.uk

Contacts in the USA

American Red Cross
19151 ST NW, Washington DC
Tel: 202 872 1304
http://www.crossnet.org/services/youth/

United Nations Association
801 Second Avenue, 2nd Floor
New York, NY 10017
Tel: 212 907 1300
email: info@unausa.org
http://www.unausa.org/

United States Fund for UNICEF
333 East 38th Street - GC-6
New York, NY 10016
Tel: 212 686 552
email: information@unicefusa.org
http://www.unicefusa.org

Contacts in Australia

Australian Red Cross
155 Pelham Street
Carlton, Vic 3053
Tel: 03 9345 1800
email: schoolprojects@nat.redcross.org.au
http://www.redcross.org.au

United Nations Youth Association
email: secretary@unya.asn.au
http://www.unya.asn.au/

UNICEF Committee of Australia
PO Box A 2005
Sydney South, NSW 1235
Tel: 61 2 9261 2811
email: unicef@unicef.org.au
http://www.unicef.com.au

Contacts in New Zealand

New Zealand Red Cross
69 Molesworth Street
Thorndon
Wellington 6038
Tel: 04 472 3750
email: national@redrcross.org.nz
http://www.redcross.org.nz/

United Nations Youth Association NZ
PO Box 12324
Wellington
Tel: 64 04 473 0441
email: info@unyanz.co.nz
http://www.unyanz.co.nz/

New Zealand Committee for UNICEF
PO Box 10987
Wellington
Tel: 64 4 473 0879
email: 2helpkids@unicef.org.nz
http://www.unicef.org.nz

Contacts in Canada

Canadian Red Cross Society
National Office
170 Metcalfe Street
Ottawa, On K2P 2P2
Tel: 613 740 1900
email: info@redcross.ca
http://www.redcross.ca/

United Nations Association in Canada
Suite 900, 130 Slater Street
Ottawa, On K1P 6E2
Tel: 613 232 5751
email: info@unac.org
http://www.unac.org/

Canadian UNICEF Committee
Canada Square
2200 Yonge Street, Suite 1100
Toronto, On M4S 2C6
Tel: 416 482 4444
email: secretary@unicef.ca
http://www.unicef.ca

Contacts in Ireland

Irish Red Cross
16 Merrion Square
Dublin 2
Tel: 353 1 676 5135
email: redcross@iol.ie
http://www.redcross.ie/

Irish National Committee for UNICEF
28 Lr Ormond Quay
Dublin 1
Tel: 353 1 878 3000
email: info@unicef.ie
http://www.unicef.ie

Other contacts

The International Criminal Tribunal for the former Yugoslavia
http://www.un.org/icty/glance/index.htm

The International Criminal Tribunal for Rwanda
http://www.ictr.org/

United Nations High Commissioner for Refugees
http://www.unhcr.ch/cgi-bin/texis/vtx/home

Glossary

accord
agreement or treaty between nations

ally
person or state whom you agree to join with in defence, or against a common enemy

armament
tools used in defence from others or to attack others

atomic bomb
type of nuclear weapon which breaks the bonds that tie atoms together releasing an immense amount of energy

battle
fight between enemies who each mean to gain a strategic advantage. Other sorts of fights are raids and sieges.

biological warfare
warfare that uses germs (bacteria or viruses) to make the enemy ill or to kill the enemy

capitalism
economic system based on private ownership (by business, industry etc.) rather than on public, or government ownership

Cathar
member of a religious group in late 12th and early 13th century southern Europe

cavalry
soldiers who fight primarily on horseback

ceasefire
agreement by both sides in a conflict to stop fighting. Ceasefires are usually temporary.

chemical weapon
weapon that uses poison to make the enemy ill or to kill the enemy

civilian
person who is not in the armed forces

Commonwealth of Nations
the British Commonweath of Nations is a voluntary association of independent nations, most of which used to be ruled by Britain

communism
economic system based on public, or government ownership, rather than that of business, or private ownership

convention
treaty agreed by several nations

cult
religious group set up to gain money or power for its leaders

dictator
ruler who is not restricted by laws and will not tolerate official opposition

ethnic group
group of people who share a common culture, a common language or believe they share a common ancestry

genocide
deliberate killing of a nation of people or an ethnic group

guerrilla
person who fights in secret against a more powerful enemy

heretical
idea which goes against accepted religious teaching

hoplite
Classical Greek armoured foot soldier

hydrogen bomb
type of nuclear weapon in which atoms of hydrogen are fused together to produce helium. Hydrogen bombs are more powerful than atomic bombs.

Industrial Revolution
change during the 18th and 19th centuries from an agricultural to an industrial economy

irregulars
soldiers who follow looser rules than regulars

just cause
policy or idea which is right

just war
war that it is right to fight

League of Nations
organization formed in 1920 to encourage nations to settle their differences peacefully

massacre
killing of many people

merchant ship
ship intended to carry passengers and cargo

militia
people who are organized to fight, but are not part of regular armies (see below)

NATO
North Atlantic Treaty Organization, formed in 1949 as an alliance of Western European nations plus Iceland, the USA and Canada. The NATO countries promise to defend each other against threats from other nations.

Nazi Germany
Germany when it was controlled by the National Socialist German Workers' Party (between 1934 and 1945)

peacekeeper
soldier sent to keep soldiers from other countries from fighting, usually as part of a United Nations peacekeeping mission

PLO
Palestinian Liberation Organization, formed in 1964 from a union of several Arab groups, with the aim of creating a state for Palestinian Arabs and removing the State of Israel

refugee
person seeking refuge from war or persecution

regular armies
armies of soldiers who are expected to follow rules. Regular soldiers are generally paid, and fight for their own countries.

reservist
civilian who is trained to join a regular army in times of emergency

shell
munition designed to be fired from an artillery piece – a large gun

Soviet Union
Union of Soviet Socialist Republics or Soviet Union was formed in 1922 from the former Russian Empire. The Soviet Union was dissolved in 1991.

systematic
according to a plan

telegraph
means of communication by electrical impulses sent over wires

terrorism
deliberate and systematic murder, maiming and menacing of the innocent to inspire fear for political ends

terrorist
person who used terrorism

theologian
person who discusses the nature of God

transfer of population
also called 'ethnic cleansing'. Forcibly moving a group of people from one area to another for political reasons.

treaty
agreement between nations

tribunal
court, usually military

truce
ceasefire

United Nations
voluntary association of countries which join together to promote international peace and security

war
conflict intended to achieve political aims by using armed forces to attack and destroy an enemy's resources or armed forces

war crime
violation of the laws of war, or a crime against humanity (such as genocide) committed during war

Index